A Book of Messages in the Form of Poems

CAN I GET AN AMEN?

Darren F Longuemire, Sr.

Copyright © 2019, 2025 by Darren F Longuemire, Sr.

All rights reserved. No part of this book may be reproduced, stored, or transmitted by any means—whether auditory, graphic, mechanical, or electronic—without written permission of both publisher and author, except in the case of brief excerpts used in critical articles and reviews. Unauthorized reproduction of any part of this work is illegal and is punishable by law.

Library of Congress Control Number: 2019903535

ISBN: 979-8-89419-653-4 (sc)
ISBN: 979-8-89419-654-1 (hc)
ISBN: 979-8-89419-655-8 (e)

Because of the dynamic nature of the Internet, any web addresses or links contained in this book may have changed since publication and may no longer be valid. The views expressed in this work are solely those of the author and do not necessarily reflect the views of the publisher, and the publisher hereby disclaims any responsibility for them.

One Galleria Blvd., Suite 1900, Metairie, LA 70001
(504) 702-6708

Dear Readers,

I would like to express my deepest gratitude to the readers and supporters of my first book. I hope you enjoy it. It's been a long time coming, but in the sight of the Lord, it's right on time. I say that because I realize that God's timing is for our benefit. I would have liked for this book to have been finished a while ago. But God's timing is what's going to make this book successful. We all have been blessed with a gift. Often, we sit our gifts on a shelf, then search for things that are right in our face.

I believe that this is the season for believers to make known the gift that God has given us and let it shine for the world to see. When you think of the many talents that you may have, the one you do that's simple, is most likely God's gift to you. We as believers know that God's best gift is His Son Jesus. Keep in mind that God won't give us gifts that are not righteous in behavior.

I would like to bring to the readers attention that all poems are not based on actual scripture. Although I have no intentions, in any way, of leading one away from the truth, I use imagination in some of my poems. For instance, I know that there won't be any loved ones waiting for us at a gate. I'm sure that in Heaven, God won't have us looking or even thinking about anything or anybody that would interrupt our joy. Everyone in Heaven will be our loved ones. Our new thoughts will not be like our old thoughts.

So, readers if you can try to look at the positive side of this book, then let this book motivate you. It is meant to be a book of inspiration, I pray that it accomplishes just that. So, if my grammar seems to be beneath your vocabulary, try to enjoy the humor of it. I'm aware that some of the words could have been properly worded, but that's what makes this book different from so many others.

Just kick back, relax and see if you can relate to some of this Christian humor CAN I GET AN AMEN?

I COULDN'T IMAGINE

I couldn't imagine having a crown full of
thorns, forced on top of my head
Or being beat with a whip, meat snatched from my
back, until my body was bloody red

Rocks thrown by the crowd, hair snatched from
my beard, even spit in my face
No, I couldn't imagine for the life of me, being in Jesus place

I couldn't imagine walking up a hill and some jokers tripping me down
And all the time carrying a cross on my back, weighing over 200 pounds

I couldn't imagine even finishing that walk, that walk-up Calvary hill
But Jesus did it for you and me, because His love is just that real

I couldn't imagine taking nails in my hands or
letting them drive nails in my feet
He didn't really have to let them do it, but
His mission wasn't quite complete

I couldn't imagine being raised on a cross, hung for all to see
But Jesus did it way up the mountain, on a hill called Calvary

I couldn't imagine staying up there so long
then being speared in the side
Or asking God to forgive them, they know not what they
do. Say it is finished, hung His head and died
I couldn't imagine raising up in three days claiming
all power in heaven and earth
Saving mankind from a burning hell, being
triumphant and rejoicing with myrrh

I couldn't imagine taking the abuse that he took or
going through what he went through
No, I couldn't imagine for the life of me, could you imagine it being you?

THE CHRISTIAN STRUGGLE

As we start to grow on our spiritual walk
we start to acknowledge our sins
So, we pray to God to fix our unbelief
so, we won't repeat them again

And even though He delivers us from some of our sins
some we cling on to
It's not that God can't deliver us from them all
but some work He leaves for us to do

God don't force us to live His way
the choice is up to us
we have to decide on this Christian journey
On whom to put our trust

We know that sometime the walk gets hard
the hills get hard to climb
but if we call on the one that has all the strength
He's our guaranteed safety line

We can count on Him in the midst of our struggle
to lighten our heavy load
He'll be our help, our counselor, and even our guide
to help us complete our goal

God never said that it would be easy
And he proved it when He gave His only son
And as hard as that walk up the hill was for Jesus
He never stopped until the victory was won

I know sometimes the walk gets a little hard
It was hard for Jesus to
but as Christians we have to learn to take a little something
like Jesus took it for me and you

CHRISTIAN FIGHT

I'm not trying to judge your life, but you make it plain to see
That when you're going through a struggle
You give up to easily

You don't seem to know who to give your problems to
You don't know that Jesus is the one that will bring you through

Stop walking around with your head hanging
down, like you're on the losing team
You can't lose with the one you choose
Because you're a child of the King

Jesus know that we fall down, but we get back up again,
He knows there's not a person on this earth
That is truly free from sin

Everyday is another day, to try to get some wrong things right
And regardless how hard your struggle is,
Don't give up the fight.

WAKE UP AND KEEP IT REAL

Wake up and keep it real, you're not sin free,
You're not that perfect Christian, you want the folks to see.

Wake up and keep it real, can you cast the first stone?
Because if you can, your saying, you never done wrong.

Wake up and keep it real, evaluate yourself,
Stop wasting time judging someone else.

Wake up and keep it real, you ain't fooling Christ,
He the only one who truly knows, who been naughty or nice

Wake up and keep it real, you been sleeping way too long
If you're going to serve the Lord, you can't keep doing wrong

Wake up and keep it real, judgement day is near
I never knew you, are the words you pray that you don't hear

Wake up and keep it real, one day this life will end
And if you don't have your house in order then you won't make it in.

SOMETHING I CAN SHARE

I had a piece of pie, that pie was very good
I'd share that pie with everyone, only if I could
There was not enough, not enough to share
I could give a few folks some, but to others it wouldn't be fair

Then I had a peach, that peach was very sweet
If someone was to taste that peach they would want more to eat
But there was only one, with many mouths to feed
I would need a lot more than one to meet the people's needs

Then there is Gods word, that truly touch my heart
This is something that all that want is welcome to a part
It tells about His mercy, It tells about His grace
This is better than peaches and pie, just come on and have a taste

There will always be enough, a supply that never ends
Enough to share with all that want, so go tell your family and friends

You'll want to keep on sharing, you'll want the world to know
You had a taste of God's sweet love, so share and watch it grow.

THE POWER OF THE BIBLE

In the beginning we read the word
And this is what help us to grow
Reading the word tells us the truth
About things God wants us to know

There's no better way that you can grow
Then to read Gods Holy Word
The Bible is all the help you need
Regardless of what you heard

If you think back, to what it took
To get you where you are today
It's going to take that same thing
That's going to make you want to stay

It's the Bible, God's instructions
On how your soul can be saved
It tells us how Jesus loved us so much
His life for us He gave

This power of the Bible, it opens up eyes
And it helps you realize the truth
It gives you a relationship with the living God
But don't take my word, read it yourself
That's where you'll find the proof

I'M GRATEFUL GOD

I'm grateful God for all you've done
You sacrificed your only son
And you did this for me, that my soul may be saved
I'm grateful God for this gift that you gave

I'm grateful God for the breath of life
My mother, my father, children and wife
I'm grateful for the roof over my head
And I'm among the living when I could have been dead

I'm grateful God that you opened my eyes
Another day you allowed me to rise
I'm grateful God to be in my right mind
And for you forgiving me time after time

I'm grateful God for your grace and mercy
You give me these gifts even though I'm not worthy
I'm grateful God for common sense
And for sending your son to be at my defense

I'm grateful God for unseen protection
When I was heading in the wrong direction
I'm grateful God for all that you've done
But I'm grateful most for your only Son

HUMILITY

Why should I show concern for your needs
When you show no concern for mine

Why should I always speak to you
When you ignore me every time

Why should I humble myself because
You want things your way

When your way don't line up with God's way
Do that still make it okay

Why do I feel like I'm showing weakness
When I give into these things that I do

Because Jesus did all these things for you
And if you love him you'd do it to

You do it to show that Jesus lives in you
And for Jesus you won't be moved

As long as you do this in the name of Jesus
For man you have nothing to prove

IT'S HARD TO BE HUMBLE

It's hard to be humble, and folks think its weakness
And you try to be peaceful with humility and meekness

It's hard to be humble, when you're being disrespected
And violence seems to be the only way to correct it

It's hard to be humble, when folk call you names
And because you love them they think your insane

It's hard to be humble, when folk hear one side
And they start to judge because some sinner lied

It's hard to be humble, when they smile in your face
Then talk about you soon as you leave the place

It's hard to be humble, when you give to the needy
But instead it gets took by the wealthy and greedy

It's hard to be humble, when you're trying to save souls
But heaven just don't seem to be some people goal

It's hard to be humble, when you're doing it alone
But if you lean on Jesus he'll keep you strong

SOMETIMES IT GETS HARD

Sometimes it's not easy, walking this Christian walk
It gets a little hard sometimes
When evil is present on every hand
The hills can get hard to climb

Sometimes it's hard to humble yourself
Or be the one to turn the other cheek
These days people take that as a sign of weakness
Instead of a man being humble and meek

Sometimes it gets hard to love, your so-called enemies
When you know they don't care about you
But that's what separates you from the world
So you can't live like they do

Sometimes it's not easy to forgive your brother
When he continues to do you wrong
It's never easy when you do it yourself
But with Christ you can always be strong

Sometimes it's hard to say I love you
When you criticize me behind my back
We got to remember in spite of their ways
We can't let them take us off track

Sometimes it's hard to say I'm sorry
Especially when I know that I'm right
When you do the things that keeps the peace
You are right in God's eye sight

WHAT IS YOUR WORD WORTH

If you needed someone to vouch for you
Could you find someone to do it
And when you give someone your spoken word
How often do you stick to it

Do you make promises you can't keep
And kind of hope for the best
And when the promise don't come through
like you hoped it would, you just make up any mess

How important is it that your word is kept
And what is your word worth to you
If someone else was to give their word
Wouldn't you expect for them to follow through

Your word should be as good as money
Something that people can trust
And whenever you give someone your word
To follow up on it, is a must

Most would be honored to honor your favors
Because of the many favors you have given
And they know that your word can truly be trusted
They've seen the life you been living

So, tell me what, is your word worth
And how important is it for you to keep
Well ask the little boy who use to cry wolf
Until he lost all of his sheep

Say what you mean and mean what you say
Your word should be like money in the bank
Your word should be like a house that's built on a rock
Not one that's built on sand that will sank

I CAN'T FORGET

I can't forget how you made a way
For me to fall on my knees and pray

I was lost in a world of sin
But you touched my heart and my praise begin

I CAN'T FORGET HOW YOU SAVED MY SOUL
When you shed your blood to make me whole

I remember the multitude you fed
You walked on water and raised the dead

I can't forget how you died for me
On that hill they call Calvary

I'm so glad to be a child of the King
The one who can fix anything

I can't forget how you left one day
And when you left, you sent the Holy Spirit our way

I want to thank you for all you've done
And thank you for the victory we already won

I can't forget all the love you shown
Even when I continue to live life wrong

I can't forget how you took me in
You pardon me from all my sins

I can't forget all you done for me
When you died for me on Calvary

TO GOD BE THE GLORY

To God be the glory
He deserves all the praise
And I will glorify him
For the rest of my days

To God be the glory
All honor is due
His grace is efficient
And His mercy is to

To God be the glory
No other can claim
To raise the dead
Or heal the lame

To God be the glory
No one can compare
To love like He loves
Or to care like He cares

To God be the glory
Don't glorify man
Man, can't fix the things
God can

To God be the glory
We can't do it alone
With God's help
We can't go wrong

To God be the glory
And he's worthy to be praised
And I will always praise Him
Until my dying days

EXAMINE YOURSELF

Examine yourself, that's where it starts
If you want to see a change, first do your part

Examine yourself, it may be your fault
Go to the one, that you may have an aught

Examine yourself, we make mistakes
Humble yourself, if that's what it takes

Examine yourself, you're a child of the King
Through Jesus Christ, you can do all things

Examine yourself, not according to others
Set an example, for your sisters and brothers

Examine yourself, you know right from wrong
Take the stripe, and keep marching on

Examine yourself, stop looking at them
Christ is the answer, focus on Him

When I examine myself, I can clearly see
The thing I need to work on most, is me

LET GO AND GROW

There's been problems in our past
That some folk can't let go
And because we hold on to the past
It's hard for us to grow

How can we be on one accord
When we allow Satan to keep us apart
Maybe it's because pleasing God
Is not truly in our hearts

We need to let go of whatever it is
That keeps us from growing closer to Christ
We need to let go of our old sins
That was a part of our old worldly life

But now that we say we know the Lord
Is it safe to say, He know us to
Because what we don't want to hear on judgement day
Is when He say to us, I never knew you

WHO YOU LIVING FOR

We live our lives as Christian Soldiers, one day at a time

But how often is the work of Christ, truly on our minds

How often do we tell the world, about the God we serve

Why is it when the opportunity is there, we sometimes lose our nerves

And even when were in God's church, we reluctant to praise and shout

When we know that worship and praising God, is what church is about

Sometimes we don't even hear the word, because we often just sit and nod

How we ever going to learn like that, on how to please our God

We live our lives as Christian Soldiers, I wonder if the world can tell

That we praise a God that saved our souls, from a burning hell

I can only imagine when this life is over, and all our work is through

What if, we hear God say those most dreadful words,

Depart I never knew you

I BELIEVE

I believe when I wake from this final sleep
I'd wake up at the foot of God's throne
I believe that I'll be welcome with open arms
And made instantly to feel at home

I believe that Paul describes it best
When he said to die is to gain
And the service I've done on this earth for the Lord
Was never done in vain

I believe I had to go through some things
But Job went through some things too
And just like Job my faith wasn't moved
I did what God told me to do

So, celebrate my going home
Don't see this as a lost
I finally went home to paradise
Because Jesus paid the cost

STAND UP MEN OF CANDLE LIGHT

Stand up men of Candle Light if your ready
to join this Christian fight

Let's pick up our flag, that blood stained banner
let's carry it around, in a military manner

We lift our flag, we hold it high
for God we live, for God we die

Let's put on our armor and pick up our sword
time is now to serve the Lord

Stop looking at the man next to you
just do what God will have you to do

It's a personal thing to serve the Lord
let's do it and be on one accord

In this army we can't lose
As long as God is on the side we choose

So, stand up men of Candle Light
it's time to join the Christian fight
put on your armor and lift your sword
time is now to serve the Lord

THE FRONT LINE

When God give us a position
We can't take the position light
As leaders we have to let the Holy Spirit lead us
If we want to do right

But it all starts on the front line
And the way we work with our sisters and brothers
If we would allow the Holy Spirit to lead us
We would truly show respect to one another

But we can't think of our self as the leader
We got to know that were truly being led
Because if we work under the leadership of God Holy Spirit
We'd have no problems doing what he said

But it all starts on the front line
To let others see us work in unity
Because if they see us working on one accord
The Holy Spirit would truly run free

It starts when we work as one
But our thinking has to be the same
We have to know with out a shadow of a doubt
What we are doing is in Jesus name

But it all starts on the front line
And which spirit you're gonna listen to
Are you going to do the things that pleases God
Or do the things that pleases you?

UNDER SURVEILLANCE

It seems no one's watching
It seems like your all alone
It looks like you can get away with it
But in your heart, you know it's wrong
No one would probably notice
How much would it cost
What profits me to gain the world
If my soul is lost
We're constantly under surveillance
And there's no place we can hide
He even knows our deepest thoughts
We think we hid inside
Don't think you're getting over
Don't think you're getting away
Everything you ever done
Will be shown on judgement day
Were constantly under surveillance
And all will be revealed
Every single deed and thought
You thought you had concealed
God knows were not perfect
He knows were going to sin
That's why He gave us Grace and Mercy
Time and time again
Don't think you're getting over
Don't think you got Him fooled
Were constantly under surveillance
He knows our every move

NEW YEAR SERVANT

Another year has come and gone
Praise God you brought me through
Many have gone home to live in glory
Praise God their home with you

Don't let my faith remain the same
I'm praying that you make it stronger
And don't let my patience be short
I'm praying you make it longer

Teach me to show kindness to all
Even when I'm not treated the same
Help me to accept responsibility for myself
And not make others the blame

Give me joy knowing, I'm a child of God
Peace in the midst of the storm
Patience to help me hold out
When I'm weary and worn

Wisdom Lord, when I'm confused
And sight when I can't see
Courage Lord, when I'm afraid
And more Grace and more Mercy

These are some of the things I need
Just to do your will
If I can't have them all, I'll try to do it still

LISTEN TO HIM

We're making choices on our own
We're not listening to the Holy Spirit
Because when it comes to listening to what He say
We just don't want to hear it

It's not the way we want it to be
It's not to our satisfaction
So instead of doing what pleases Christ
We go the other direction

Why can't we do the right thing
And move self out the way
All the bad choices we make on earth
Will be revealed on judgement day

We say we love the Lord
Because he heard our cry
He also heard us reject His word
And he also heard our lies

But the choice is ours to make
Who do we want to please
Who is the one we give thanks to
When we go down on our knees

We got to make better decisions
we can't keep choosing our way
we got to start listening to the Holy Spirit
and when we hear Him we got to obey

So, the next time we come to that fork in the road
and we're faced with making a decision
we got to listen to the voice that bring Christians together
and not the voice that causes division…

READ THE INSTRUCTION

The instructions are all that we need
They don't need to be arranged
They don't need help from no other book
It just wouldn't be the same

Sometimes you might ask the question
Why don't some churches grow
Sometime the preachers don't tell the people
The things God wants them to know

Some preachers use words that are too sophisticated
Sometime the people don't understand
That's not the way you save the people souls
Although they may sound impressive to man

You ask why the churches aren't growing
Some preachers don't preach from their hearts
Some churches have clicks that keep to themselves
And that usually keep a church split apart

But it all falls on the leader
And how he follows God's instructions
As long as he's doing it the way God tell him to
He'll be able to pray out interruptions

The instructions are meant to be followed
Without them your soul would be lost
And if we don't follow them correctly
In hell is where our souls will be tossed

So, do what you need to
To get the instructions right
But you got to be armed with the word
To continue the Christian fight

BLESSINGS

I counted ten blessings, before I got out of bed
He didn't have to wake me, I could have been dead

He opened my eyes, so that I can see
Consumers didn't turn off my electricity

Heard my wife snoring, so I know she was breathing
No calls through the night, that had me grieving

I realized I was in my right mind
When I lifted myself up, my limbs worked fine

Swung around, put my feet on the floor
Felt kind of good, my back wasn't sore

God is so good, there's no doubt about it, I know
And the good thing about it, I've got 9,990 more to go

HAVE YOU CONSIDERED

Have you considered how blessed you are
When God woke you up still in your right mind

Or to serve a God that can raise the dead
Heal the cripple, deaf and blind

Have you ever considered how loved you are
That one would die for your sins

And continue to love you and pick you up
Time after time again

Have you ever considered that the way your living
Is the way your children think its supposed to be done

So be considerate of how you live, before your loved ones
Be a good example in front of your daughters and sons

DON'T JUDGE ME

You only heard it from one person side
And now you're ready to judge
Not only have you found me guilty, you're doing it with a grudge
You look at me and roll your eyes
And I don't even know why
All I know is your attitude change, whenever I come by

They say to every story there should at least be two sides
We should always hear them both
You can't go by just one person side
Not even if they tell it under oath

We can't be getting caught up in all that he say, she say mess
People lie so much today its hard to judge the truth
That's why it's better when you witness it yourself
And make your judgement according to your proof

Don't judge me by what somebody say
You don't know how they feel about me
Take the time to get to know me yourself
That way you can judge me by what you see

Don't judge me and I won't judge you
I'll respect you by the way you show respect
And regardless what anybody else may say
The respect I've seen is what I won't forget

Don't judge me it's not your job
God already got it under control
It's not your judgement that's going to send me to heaven
Or determine the fate of my soul

If you judge me then who'll judge you
And don't think they'll judge you with grace
As for me you can judge me as much as you want
But Jesus already won my case

A BAD REPUTATION

Isn't it a shame how some people judge you
By the way you use to live

And although some people can see the change
There is others who just can't forgive

So, they continue to think the worst of you
And judge without hesitation

Judging you by the life you once lived
When you were known for having a bad reputation

There was another known for having a bad reputation
In them days he was known as Saul

He had a reputation for killing Christians
Until he got Jesus's call

And even then, the people were hesitant
Because of his past situation

God had changed his name to Paul
Because of his bad reputation

But trust and believe that one's life can be changed
When they accept Jesus in their heart

And although some folk may never accept you
With Christ you have a brand-new start

So, go ahead and start living for Jesus
Through Him you're a new creation

My God can fix any situation
Even a bad reputation

THE DEVIL IS A LIE

You know that he's a liar
Yet, sometimes he's so convincing
But getting you to believe him
Is Satan main intentions

He knows the things that bother you
So those things is what he use
He knows if he'd blind you with a lie
You'd start to falsely accuse

He builds on your insecurities
To make false things seem real
And even though you know there lies
You give into him still

He'll make you turn against your spouse
Could be husband or wife
It really don't matter which one to him
As long as he ruins your life

You know he's out like a lion
To seek whom, he can destroy
And it don't matter how he do it
As long as he steals your joy

If you want your mind at ease
Don't listen to Satan's mess
Put your trust in Jesus Christ
If you want peace and rest

FREE FROM THE WORLD

You can be free where ever you are
If you truly accept Christ in your heart
You can have joy and you can have peace
To know Christ is the start

If you take one step, God will take two
Then just watch your growth begin
You'll find out that on this Christian journey
You won't find a better friend

So be encouraged, God is never wrong
He has work for you to do
He changes the life of many sinners
And he can change your life too

So, pull up your sleeves, get ready to work
Go ahead and spread the news
I'm no longer a prisoner of the world
But for Jesus, THE KING OF THE JEWS!!!

NO HIDING PLACE

We say that we believe in God
And we believe that He's always watching us
So why, is it so easy for us to sin
With our lies, backbiting and lust

He's always looking, He's always there
But we disrespect Him, like we just don't care
We still like to gamble, drink and get high
We live our lives like were never going to die

Now, we know that He'll wipe away our sins
And provide us with a brand-new start
But don't think that we can pull nothing over Him
He knows what's in our hearts

We're so concerned to hide from man
All the sins that we do
The main ones that we're trying to hide them from
Are probably trying to hide sins from you

Maybe the sin your stuck on wasn't mentioned
It doesn't mean that you're getting away
God knows every sin that we ever done
He'll show us on judgement day

Now, no one is excluded from sin
God knows that were not perfect
But we got to keep putting our trust in Him
In the end we'll see that He was worth it

MY WORST ENEMY

The enemy is always working, even when I'm sleep
When he makes his plans for me, he makes them by the week

He's got my routine down, he knows just how I think
And because of the way he operates, sometimes he makes life stink

But now I got his number, I know how he thinks too
And since I know how he thinks, there's some changes I must go through

I can't destroy this enemy, because he's like no one else
And there's no way I can bring him harm, without bringing harm to myself

By now you're probably wondering, who can this enemy be
Well of all the enemies I ever had, my worst enemy is ME

Yes, I've done more harm to me, that anyone has ever done
And if I was to put my enemies in order, I'd be number one

But thank God there's an answer, and His name is Jesus Christ
And I know if I move out the way, he'll make everything alright

Jesus said it's not my battle, it's much too hard for me
He said if I didn't feed the flesh, I would destroy the enemy

The flesh is my evil side, some people call it Satan
And as long as I continue to feed the flesh,
you can bet He'll be there waiting

So, I got to stop feeding the flesh, because the flesh is my worst enemy
And I don't need no enemy, trying to direct my life for me

PRESSING PASS OUR CONVICTIONS

We are pressing pass our convictions
Although we know that we are sinning
We're causing Jesus sorrow
But we got the devil grinning

We're pressing pass our convictions
But we claim that we are saved
We need to take more time to learn
How a Christian should behave

We're pressing pass our convictions
With sins that we block out
The sins that we purposely hold on to
Some of you know what I'm talking about

We're pressing pass our convictions
Because were weak to our strong holds
But there's power in the Word of God
We just got to let Him take control

We're pressing pass our convictions
Because we like the sin we be doing
But we got to put them in the Lord's Hands
If it's righteousness we're truly pursuing

We're pressing pass our convictions
But we got to press to do right
We got to press to do God's will
So, all may be well in God's sight

OTHER PEOPLES BLESSING

In the midst of recognizing other people's blessings
Don't forget to recognize your own
Sometimes we take our blessings for granted
Like our health, our strength, our home

Sometimes we don't acknowledge our families unbroken circle
We just assume that it's a natural thing
But please believe it's truly a blessing
Because we know not what tomorrow will bring

We always thinking that others' lives are better
Or, I want to live like their living
But just because things look good from our eyes
To hell, their soul, they may be giving

Because it really doesn't matter about material things
What really matter is peace with in
What really matter is knowing that Christ is the answer
And with Him you won't find a better friend

In the midst of recognizing other folk's blessings
Know that all blessings don't come from above
Know that all blessings don't have to be material things
The best blessing that we could ever have has to be Jesus love

ARE YOU BLESSED

Start acting like your blessed

Stop crying broke all the time

You cry broke as a habit

And its stuck up in your mind

You act like God don't bless you

But working nearly everyday

Maybe you ought to evaluate

How you spend your pay

You say you give your tithes

Do you give them from your heart

If you're not giving 10%

I truly suggest that you start

You can't beat God's giving

No matter how hard you try

Because whatever you give in Jesus name

He can ten times multiply

Start acting like your blessed

You're a child of the King

What you crying for

Your Dad owns everything, Amen

MAKING PLANS AND DYING

No one seen it coming
It took us by surprise
We're making plans for later
But God controls our lives

No one knew the future
Hour, night or day
No one's time is guaranteed
Unless God say it's okay

We're making plans and dying
Because we know that day will come
And for many it will happen
Not always true for some

No need for you to worry,
It's in the Master hands
Take time out to learn,
About Gods' salvation plan

So go ahead and plan
But say, if it's Gods will
Because any plans God has for you
It is stamped, signed and sealed

Don't worry about tomorrow
This day is not yet through
There's still a chance to know Gods' plan
It's really up to you

We're making plans and dying
There's many that's not prepared
It's not too late to know Gods plans
That your soul from hell, be spared

FORGETFUL CHRISTIANS

We all know them by their fruits
But it's not our job to judge

Because you know when we start pointing fingers
We do it with a grudge

We think and call them sinners
As if we never do

But know that while we're judging others
We're also being judged to

We can't judge ourselves so righteous
Based on what folks do

There was a time when some of us
Use to drink and raise hell to

But now that we've calmed down
Their sins seem so wrong

But it didn't seem to be so wrong
When we were doing it on our own

Everyone should have a privilege
To be a living testimony

Don't think that because God showed you grace and mercy
That it was meant for you, only

PASSING THEM OUT

He's passing out blessings, you better get yours

He's casting out demons, and opening up doors

He's passing out blessings, no waiting in line

His only requirement, have a made-up mind

Know that He's able, trust and believe

And wait on the blessings, your about to receive

He's passing out blessings, 10,000 a day

All you got to do, is ask when you pray

It may not come, as fast as you like

But when it comes, the time will be right

He's passing out blessings, He'll never run out

Just know that it's coming, without any doubt

He's passing out blessings, to the crippled, the blind

He won't give me yours, and He won't give you mines

He's passing out blessings, but you got to believe

And through Jesus Christ, you shall receive

OVER FLOW OF PRIDE

So much pride is coming out of our ears,
But that's not the way it should be
So many of us call ourselves a child of God,
But we take side with the enemy

One of the sins God hates the most
Is one who is lifted in pride
So why do we act the way that displeases Him
When we say were on His side

We'll hold up our blessing to get our way
Instead of humbling our self like the bible say
So much pride, we'd walk alone
Instead of telling our loved one, we were wrong

Some of us are so lifted in pride
We'd rather walk up front
Instead of by one's side

So much pride we can't take directions
It's my way or no way
With no exceptions

So full of pride we can't give in for right
And we know it's a sin
In Jesus sight

Why do we think it's all about us
When Jesus shows us
Its Him we can trust

Why can't we just swallow our pride
And move out the way
and let Jesus in side

We should pray for the spirit of humility
So, we can all work in unity
And act the way that God would be pleased
With prayer we can defeat our enemies

WORLD FLESH DEVIL

LIAR

You're a liar
And everybody knows it
You're a liar
It's like you can't control it

You're a liar
It's not even necessary
You're a liar
Trusting you is kind of scary

You're a liar
One of Gods most hated sins
You're a liar
It's gonna hurt you in the end

You're a liar
You better pray about it
You're a liar
If you want to live without it

You're a liar
But you don't have to be
Trust in God
And He'll give you victory

NEXT TIME

It happened to them, it didn't happen to us
So, we don't feel their pain
It wasn't our child that got shot down
To us, life remains the same

But to remain the same means to worry
Next time will someone kill mine
It's getting hard to let our kids go out
But we can't keep them home all the time

It happened to them, not us
So why should we take a stand
Maybe we should wait until it happens to us
Before we try to come up with a plan

Some people think that the kids that are dying
Are kids that are always doing wrong
But that wasn't the case of the nine-year-old boy
And the six-year-old, Layla Jones

But it happened to them, it didn't happen to us
So why should we get involved
Even though we know that's what it takes
To get these crimes resolved

Just like it happened to them one day
It could happen to you

JEALOUS SEED

Satan planted a jealous seed, way in the back of my mind
And it didn't seem to grow at first, but he knew that it would in time

You see, he watered it down with imagination
of lies your mind tells your heart
And although in your mind you don't truly believe,
but this is when the growing first start

Every now and then, you think of the lies, and think, what if that's true
This is the next stage of the seed, that Satan has planted in you

You try to be strong, but Satan is stronger, you can't handle Him alone
Now Satan got you asking her questions, every time that she leave home

Where are you going, when will you be back
You got her wondering why your tripping like that

In time, the seed has turned into a tree
Your mind is infested with jealousy

You never use to think these crazy thoughts before
Satan has touched you, and made you insecure

At times like this you truly need a reliever
To save you from this Satanic deceiver

Trust in Jesus, and in time you'll find
He can remove that seed from the back of your mind

Remember that Satan is out to destroy
And He knows what to use, to steal your joy

FULLY FURNISHED

There's a mansion up there, built just for me
And it was finished just the other day
So, when Jesus came and told me it was done
I move in right away

It's fully furnished, with all that I need
I didn't have to bring a thing
I also was given this bright white robe
I've never seen clothes so clean

The pain I had before I left
No longer lives in me
And I must admit I use to worry
But now I'm worry free

If there ever was a time to shout
Then you should shout for me
I've gone home to live in glory
Just where I want to be

WORDS FROM AN ANGEL

If only you knew how great heaven is
Then you wouldn't cry for me

Instead you will try to be prepared
So that you could come and see

I don't have that broken body
I used to have before

And I don't feel the pains and worries
Thank God not anymore

Life on earth was good to me
But Heaven is so much better

Thank God he finally brought me home
To have joy and peace forever

So, dry your eyes, God is good
And don't cry for me

I'm finally home in the bosom of Jesus
Just where I want to be

So, I won't say goodbye
Instead I'll see you in awhile

And when God bless you to be with me
I'll greet you with a smile

I'M READY

You knew the life I lived
You knew I've been preparing

You knew that the Word of God
Is what I loved most sharing

I know that I'll be missed
But only for a while

One day you'll be coming home
And I'll greet you with a smile

So please don't mourn to long
I'm where I'd rather be

If you keep on living life for God
Then one day you will see

There's no greater feeling
Than being around God's throne

Singing with the Angel's
Thank God I'm finally home.

HOME WITH THE ANGELS

We ought to be giving God praise
He calls His angels home
She now has peace and unspeakable joy
While she sings around the throne

Jesus prepared her mansion in heaven
Just like He said He would
Now that she's done had a taste of heaven
She wouldn't come back if she could

The memories of the loved ones we lose
Are the reason our heart hurts with pain
But when you know about God she served
Her serving was not in vain

So, go ahead and shout, the angels are singing
Yes, their singing around God's throne
Jesus has finished her mansion in heaven
It was time for her to go home

We ought to be giving God praise
That he called his angel home
Singing around the throne with the angels
Just where she belongs

NEVER ENDING JOY

Have you ever pictured heaven in your mind
Do you ever read about it
Are you a believer that heaven exist
Or are you one of those that doubt it

The true believer know that heaven is real
And after death life just really begins
According to the bible it is a place of great joy
And it is said that the joy never ends

Even though we'll miss our loved one's smile
Their kind acts and especially their voices
So, we go on and mourn for our loved ones with heavy hearts
But for the true believers we also have to take time to rejoice

We have to recognize that God knows when to call His angels home
To that place where joy never ends
They won't have to suffer the pain and discomfort
Of their broken bodies again

We ought to be shouting Glory Hallelujah
For God allowing us to have them so long
And we ought to give God honor and praise
For bringing His servants back home

Thank you for blessing us with the loved ones you gave us
One day we'll see them again
And we'll all sing together in that Heavenly choir
In the land where joy never ends

I'LL BE LOOKING AT THE GATE

Some journeys you have to take alone
And this is one of those
Some journeys you can't choose the time
Instead you have to be chose

So, until that time come when God call your name
You'll have to be patient and wait
But as for me, I'll be praising the Lord
And looking for you at the gate

So, don't be mourning to long for me
I've prepared to be where I'm at
And although Satan tried real hard to distract my praise
Praise God I didn't look back

So, stay on that path the righteous path
The reward in heaven is great
But, as far as for me I'll be singing and shouting
And looking for you at the gate

Tell everybody about the goodness of God
And the joy felt from heaven above
In one word if I could describe that feeling
That one word would have to be love

No man knows the minute or hour
Only God knows the exact time and date
But just keep on serving and praising the Lord
And I'll be looking for you at the gate

PEACE TIME

Its peace time, for this Christian Soldier
He's fought the fight for a while
But God said put down your sword and shield
It's time to come home my child

Its peace time for this Christian Soldier
Never to fight again
Because where he's going, there'll never be war again,
only joy and peace that never ends

Its peace time for this Christian Soldier
And the believers just ought to shout
Because celebrating his home going
Is what this is all about

Its peace time for this Christian Soldier
And although our hearts may be heavy
God knows what's best for us all
He knew his soldier was ready

It's peace time for this Christian Soldier
His new life has just begun
I can hear God saying "Well done Christian Soldier"
The victory has been won

HE KNOWS

God never said it would be easy
He knows none of us is perfect
But I'll try my best to please Him
Because I know my God is worth it

He knows sometimes I'll fall short
He knows sometimes I'll stray
He knows sometimes I'll get off the road
But He knows I'm not off to stay

He knows my every weakness
And I know He hears my prayer
And I know that he'll deliver me
Because I know, He truly cares

I know that every good gift I have
come from up above
But three of the gifts I treasure most
Is His Grace, His Mercy, His Love

PROCRASTINATING SPIRIT

Procrastinating has never got me any where
It always seems to put my life on hold
And as longs I keep on procrastinating
It'll be difficult for me to reach my goals

I'm fully aware I'm doing it, when I'm doing it
But at the time my excuses seem to be legit
Sometimes my job can be my main distraction
But right now, it's too important for me to quit

I spend too much time watching television
Even though I've seen the programs many times
When I really should spend more time reading my bible
At least that would help grow my spiritual mind

Procrastinating keeps us from our blessings
It also put purpose on delay
But just because things don't go like we want them
We put our dreams on hold another day

Procrastinating, one of Satan's unspoken weapons
The silent killer of dreams
The spirit of thinking there's always tomorrow
But no man knows what tomorrow may bring

So, remember God blesses us all, with a special gift
And He leaves it up to us how to use it
So, don't get caught up in that procrastinating spirit
Procrastinating could cause you to lose it

MAKING ALL THESE BABIES

You're making all these babies
With no regards to their life
All these babies momma's
Not one of them your wife

It's completely obvious your life has no direction
You can't have much thought to your future
Having sex without protection

There's disease out here that's killing folk
I'm sure you heard of AIDS
and you can't be bright upstairs
Not to be afraid

You're probably bragging to your friends
About the sex you're having
But once you start paying child support
I bet that you won't be laughing

A guy like you with all them babies
A parent's worst nightmare
Having a daughter that's raising a baby
With a father that's never there

Making all these babies
And not working any where
How you going to feed them
I guess you just don't care

One day you'll find that someone
Shell be that special lady
But she won't give you the time of day
When she finds out you got all them babies

TEXTING TROUBLE

He looked away one second, while he was trying to text
But that was all it took for him, to cause a wreck

It could have been avoided if only he had waited
But because he tried to drive and text
Look what he created

He wasn't paying attention, that's why he ran that red light
And that great big man in the other car
Look like he wanted to fight

This time he got off lucky, this time no life was lost
But after beginning to pay all his fines
You can bet it's going to cost

As far as that big man in the other car
He too has spared your life
But you probably have a hard time
Explaining that black eye to your wife

The time it takes to type or text a phone number
Could be the time your numbers up.

ADDICTED TO FACEBOOK

I like to look on Facebook
It has many attractions
But I find myself looking on too much
Yes, it's become a distraction

I know it's a good way to communicate
With loved ones that moved far away
But there's no reason that I should be on Facebook
More than one hour each day

See I don't have time to play candy crush
Or none of them Facebook games
Now, I'm not knocking the ones that do
You have the right to do your thing

See life is too short to get caught up in these things
That will never get you anywhere
And none of us know the minute or hour
So, there's really no time to spare

You see, there are things to see, places to go
And I like to get there someday
Now, I appreciate your invitation
But I don't have time to play

I like looking on Facebook from time to time
But I won't let it be an addiction
Because when I'm putting more time in it than my Bible
I begin to feel conviction

LET ME ASK YOU SOMETHING

If one of your friends jump off a bridge
Would you jump off too
If the crowd you hang with started doing drugs
Is that something that you would do

If none of your friends never left the hood
Would you have the courage to leave
If someone told you that you wouldn't amount to nothing
Is that what you would believe

If you had a chance to set an example
Would you make your parents proud
Or would you be the kind of example
That would impress you and your crowd

If you had the chance to be successful
Would you let your friends hold you back
Or do you have the real true friend
That instead would help you pack

Do you have any plans for the future
Or will you continue to make excuses instead
In the morning do you get up to look for work
Or are you the type that spends your morning in bed

Take the time to answer these questions
The choice is yours to make
There's a dead-end road, and a road to success
Which road do you think you will take

SSI

I'm not knocking those that need it
It's meant for those that do
But for those who think their getting over
This message is just for you

Some folk call it easy money
"just act a little crazy"
And as soon as you start getting them checks
It only makes you lazy

You feel you no longer need a job
You don't look for work no more
But once you sign up for SSI
You sign up to be poor

With your monthly income about $700
And half of that is rent
Once you pay for gas and lights
You barely have a cent

Now I know some people make it happen
They know what to do to survive
But those that's trying to make real money
I say keep hope alive

Don't get caught up in the system
Of a generational curse
Waiting once a month to get paid
On the third and for some the first

I'm not knocking those that need it
It's meant for those that do
But for those that can work for a living
SSI is not for you

I'M A SUGAR ADDICT

I'm an addict, but you probably can't tell
Because what I'm addicted to, all the grocery stores sale
But I'm an addict and it's hard to quit
And what I'm addicted to is legally legit

It's not heroin or crack cocaine
Not even the pills I use to take for pain
Yes, I'm an addict and I might as well confess it
And none of my suppliers can ever be arrested

Yeah, I'm an addict and your probably one to
You are, if you eat sweets, the way that I do
I love pies, ice cream and cakes
And all sorts of cookies, especially home baked

Yes, I'm an addict and it's a doggone shame
But when I try to quit, the sweets be calling my name
I'm not going to let this addiction defeat me
I'm not going to let the devil feed me diabetes

I'm an addict and the addiction is real
Sometimes I play it off, like it's no big deal
Sometimes I eat things that I know will make me sick
But still I find myself trying, to get a sugar fix

When we talk about addiction, we think of alcohol, and crack
But being hooked to sugar can be just like that
Yes, I'm an addict, but now that I know
I really got to let all them sweets and stuff go

SUGAR DIABETES IS NO JOKE

UNMOTIVATED SON

Are you looking for a job
Because it ain't looking for you
And what kind of work
Do you think you can do

You don't have any work experience
You hardly work at home
How do you think you're going to make it
Out there on your own

You didn't finish high school
Doesn't look like you're even trying to do it
You keep saying your gonna finish
But now is the time to prove it

You really need to have a made-up mind
And don't be ashamed to pray
Tell the Lord about your struggles
You go through day-by-day

Although some things seem difficult
You should never accept defeat
Because as long as you're trying to make it
You can never say you've been beat

THE MEETING PLACE

There's a meeting place for guys like you
That like to do the dirt you do

There's a meeting place for those who can't behave
Where once again you become a slave

There's a meeting place, where the meetings are long
It may be years before you get to go home

At this meeting place you get a new ID

7778433

At this meeting it just might be a while
Before you get a chance to see you mother, wife or child

At this meeting place, the next coffee break
With good behavior may be from 2 to 8

At this meeting place, you get a new pal
His name is Big Bubba, he'll be sharing your cell

Don't come to this meeting place
Unless you want to live in a very small space

Don't come to this meeting place
It may be the last time you see your mother's face

If you choose to keep on following trouble
Just remember your next meeting place may be with Big Bubba

He'll leave the light on for you